Drawing BIRDS

By

Rajni & Ajay

UNICORN BOOKS

ISBN: 978-81-7806-129-0 © Publishers
UNICORN BOOKS Pvt. Ltd., J-3/16, Darya Ganj, New Delhi-110002
Phones: 23276539, 23272783/84, Fax: 23257790
E-mail: unicornbooks@vsnl.com
Website: www.unicornbooks.in • www.kidscorner.in

Contents

Introduction

This book is about making you happy and taking you on a great adventure. As you go though its pages, you will become more aware about the wonderful world of birds. You will find that they are one of the most fascinating subjects to draw. So just pick up that pencil of yours and start drawing these beautiful creatures. Set aside any so-called rules and follow your intuition and interest. Draw for yourself and for your pleasure. Praise and appreciation will come as your drawing improves. All it needs is a keen interest in the subject, for the time being. Knowledge and perfection will come with practice.

Circles and ovals are the basic shapes to draw any bird. The difference and variation among them lies in the formation of the neck and beak. Always start the day with drawing a number of circles free hand on a rough page. As you can see in these drawings of Duck, the big oval shape is used for the main body and the small circle for the head. In some cases you don't even need to draw the neck. Hooded Merganser Duck is one fine example of what we want to say.

Mallard

Hooded Merganser

4

Eyes, head and the texture which is typical to the bird concerned should be the point of interest. See the drawing of Bufflehead Duck here and note the dark feathers on top of the head, on the back and the long outgoing feathers of the wing. Middle tone should now be added to define the curvature of the body and the head.

Bufflehead Duck

5

Getting Started

Budgerigars

Take a light mount or hardboard piece 10" by 12." Place a big clamp on top of it for gripping the paper. Sharpen four or five pencils. Fix ten to twelve pieces of paper to the above board. <u>Do not use an eraser.</u> Select a photo or drawing or watch the bird itself, and off you go with your pencil. Use the side of the pencil point and draw the outline in bold strokes. Add shadows and finally some details to the areas related to the focal point. All you need is to have the will to get started, from where you are right now. So practise, and just do your best. Remember to have fun while you are at it.

Take a 4B pencil and draw the circle for the body and then the line indicating neck. Add the circle for the head and the curved lines suggesting wings. Your basic drawing to sketch the above Swan is completing now. Using broad strokes fill up the shadows under the wings and on the neck. Darken the beak and the eyes. Some strokes of middle tone placed here and there will define this beautiful picture of Swan.

Swan

7

Ringneck Duck

Mallard

After placing the basic shape, add the line suggesting neck. Now define the major parts of the birds ignoring the fine details.Your bird will start appearing on the paper. Add main shadows and major dark areas and texture of the feathers. The only thing left now is the fine detail around the focal point.

8

Parrot

Flying Parrots appear like the letter K. The curves representing extended wings should be drawn keeping in mind the relative proportion of the body shape of the bird. Circle for head should be placed tilted towards the front side. Beak should be close to the chest. The long tail and the legs should be more straight and pushed towards the branch. We have used middle tone of broad strokes to define the overall body of the Parrot below. Darken the ring around the neck, eyes, beak and the parts which are hidden from the sunlight.

9

While the object we sketch is three-dimensional, our sketch can only be in two dimensions. We have to create the illusion of depth by using various techniques, e.g. shading. We use strokes, less detail and smaller size to push the object into the background. As we start adding details and defining things more clearly through strokes, the drawing will appear more realistic. Pen Grip can only produce a thin line. Other grips are used for medium to broad lines. With practice, one can also draw very fine lines with these grips. You can also do this with a sharp pencil and light pressure.

Eyes, centreline of the beak and the fine feathers should be drawn by the Pen Grip.

The big textures of the wing and the light shades of the body are more suitable for the Upper Hand Grip which is shown below.

Texture created by a stroke is another important thing in bird drawing. Above texture is of 6B pencil on textured paper with very little pressure of hand and by the Upper Hand Grip.

If you pull the pencil along with the tilt, the stroke will be very thin. Using the same pencil and keeping the same posture, draw a stroke in the cross line from the first one. You will see a more dark and broad stroke by the same pencil.

HB   2B   6B   Cross-hatch

Lower Hand Grip is most suitable for large drawings. When you are using a half drawing sheet, keep it at the arm's length and move your hand from the shoulder. You will see that the flow of the stroke will be excellent and the enjoyment unlimited. Some of the beautiful pictures in this book like Shearwater, Frigate, Golden Eagle, Emu, Hornbill and the Ostrich head are drawn by this grip. This grip is also good for rough sketches as it has more manouvring capacity than any other stroke. Once you get familiar with it, try sketching with soft pastels. On black paper, these colours give excellent results.

Another important thing is the direction of the stroke. In the examples given below you can see it for yourself. The cross-hatch and the dark, mixed strokes are used to create volume. If you want to show some fine texture or lines in drawing, then you can use either a blade, white colour or an eraser. To diffuse an area, rub your finger or a piece of cloth over it.

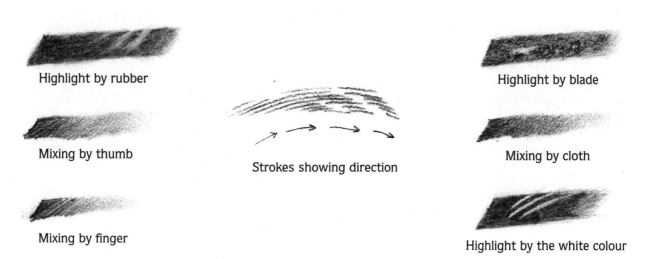

Highlight by rubber

Mixing by thumb

Mixing by finger

Strokes showing direction

Highlight by blade

Mixing by cloth

Highlight by the white colour

Casqued Hornbill

This sketch is a fine example of creating focus and diffusing other parts. We have used broad strokes applied by the side of the pencil lead to sketch in the body.

Such sketches don't have finished outlines, so although they create volume, they still feel soft as a bird should be.

When drawing this beautiful Hornbill, you have to place the circular shape meant for head more close to the egg shape of the main body. Also mark the correct place of the eyes in relation to the beak. The square type texture around the eyes is another typical feature of this bird. Draw the centreline of the beak first, then keeping in mind the difference of width between upper and lower part, draw the final shape. Increase the darkness in and around the eyes. Adding a few lines for tail and some details in eyes and head will complete the job.

Hornbill

13

The Light Effect

Light plays a very important and crucial role in creating the volume of an object. Carefully observe the source of light, its direction and the resulting shape and shadows given on this page. Every object resembles with any one of these four main shapes. In reality, the living things are a complex mixture of all these four type of shapes. As we are drawing birds here, the circular and cylindrical shapes become useful. The head and main body of a bird is of circular shape and the neck cylindrical. The tone of the shade changes with the angle and distance from the light source, and the curvature and the texture of the bird. You also have to keep in mind the type of light source. The sunlight, and the light bulb, has more focussed type of light and a diffused light is what you get from a tube light. A bird under a tree or in the shadows will appear flat in tone and contrast. The same bird flying or sitting under the sunlight will have a more pronounced shadow under it and a bright contrast of light on top of its body.

You can see what we mean if you carefully observe the given picture of Egret here. It is flying in bright sunlight. So the shadows could only fall under the wings. Other parts of the body of this small, beautiful bird are so illuminated that we have no choice but to draw them in outline only. The second Egret has even less shadows. Only the underbelly and some parts under the tail are in darkness.

The light is coming from the top on the Egret and from top right on the Falconets. See what happens when the light source changes its position and angle. The right side area of the Falconets is brightest and not the top as in the case of Egret. The left side of the Falconets has the darkest shades and the front is of middle tone. Try drawing the same bird from the different sources of light and you will learn a very important lesson in drawing birds.

Egret

Falconets

15

Drawing side view of a Sparrow is really easy. Draw a straight line for the back, turn it at the top to create head. Another straight line for the tail should then be placed a little below the first one. Connect this point with the curved line of head. Use a long, curved, boat-like stroke. Now start finishing from head, then the eyes and the beak. Work slowly and steadily. Outline, as a whole, should be drawn first. The darkest areas are eyes, top and underside of the beak joint and below the wings. Add strokes of medium tone now.

Sparrow

To draw the front or the back view of Sparrow use two circles, one for the body and other for the head. Beak and tail should then be added. Define the shaded and the lighted parts in contrast, using minimum of strokes. Middle tone is very effective in bringing out the volume and in defining the curvatures.

Erasers should be not be used. Once you erase an incorrect line, it will vanish from your mind. Also, you might repeat that mistake later. So leave it there to remind you that it is the wrong line. We learn from our mistakes, but only if we preserve them for future reference.

Marabou Stork

This big and heavy bird should be drawn in bold strokes. These birds are scavengers and have very coarse type of bodies.

Draw the big oval shape and relatively small circle for the head. Its beak is very big and heavy so it should be drawn keeping the size of the body in mind. Now finish the drawing using long, sweeping strokes. Add dark tones only at the head, around eyes and on the long feathers of the wing.

The Bulbul is a very common bird in India. It makes a short, crisp sound and keeps hopping from branch to branch. Simple shapes are always a good base to start a more complex drawing.

Spend some time in the hills and relax for a while. It will help immensely in improving your physical and mental state.

Anatomy

If you want your drawing of a bird to appear realistic, then you must have good knowledge of its anatomy. You don't have to be an expert to make a simple sketch of it but if you know what lies underneath its feathers, then you are in a better position to improve the final result.

Bone structure is nearly the same in all types of birds, so learning about it will always help you. Another important thing you should learn is the arrangement of feathers and their density and distribution patterns over the bird's body. This knowledge will prove invaluable when you draw birds in flight.

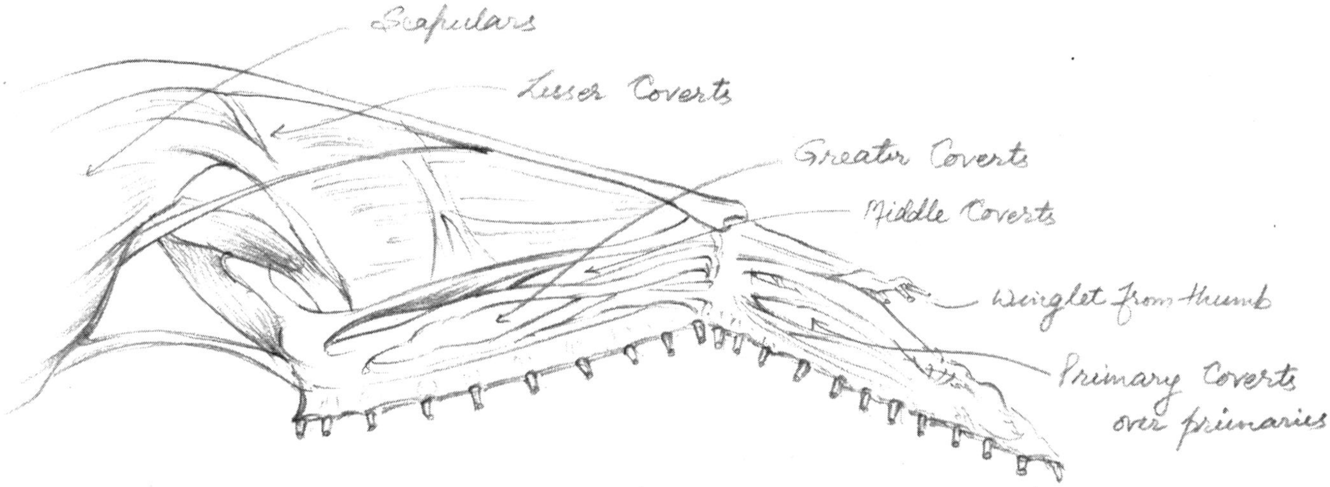

Scapulars

Lesser Coverts

Greater Coverts

Middle Coverts

Winglet from thumb

Primary Coverts
over primaries

Wing coverts

Winglet from thumb

Secondaries

Primaries

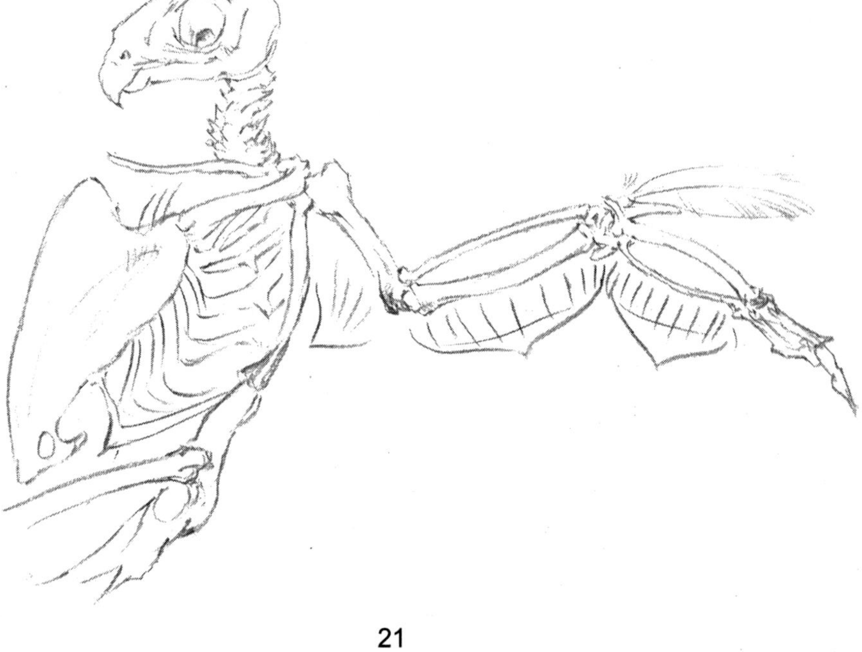

The Ostrich is the biggest bird and although it cannot fly, it can run very fast (60 miles per hour). Look at its long neck. It stands about seven feet tall. This height enables it to see things that are far away. This is very necessary for its survival, as danger constantly lurks on the vast plains of Africa.

Ostrich

For some birds like Emu only the outline done with accuracy is more effective than the dark shadows. This Emu here is a fine example of what we mean. Try adding shadows to it and you will see that a certain hardness will start appearing. Draw the big oval and two curved lines for neck and then the head, tail and the long legs. It is a big, heavy bird, so keep the angle and the size of the legs accurate. The front one is smaller than the other leg. Now start finishing from top of the head, then go to the eyes and beak. Keep working towards the neck and then the body slowly. In the beginning try to copy the strokes as they are. After some time your hand will find its own flow and choice of strokes. After finishing the body, go to the legs and complete them with minimum of lines.

Ostrich

Emu

23

Cock

Cock & Hen

Hen

Cocks are one of the best subjects to learn bird drawing. Look at the Hen in front view and looking down. Two simple circles established the creature. If you put some dark shadows under the head, it will appear more projected. Also note the direction of the strokes on various parts of the body. It is totally different on the other three birds. You have to identify it all by yourself as to which types of strokes when pulled in a certain direction can bring out what type of shape. The best way to learn it is to copy as many pictures as possible along with those given in this book.

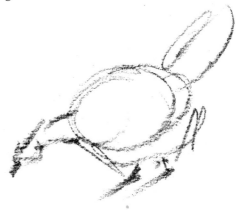

Hen

Drawing Pigeons is always a pleasure, for they are really gentle birds. Start with the simple oval shape for both the body as well as the head. Lines suggesting tail and feet should then be added. Now finish the body and wings in broad strokes, using the side of the pencil. Add detail to the eyes, beak and head. Look all over the figure once more, and add a few strokes to finish the drawing. Be extra careful when drawing the curvature of its neck. It is very different from that of other birds. Head and beak form a triangle. The lower neck is like a Duck's, its head is like a Hen's and it moves like an Egret.

Pigeon

26

Treecreeper

This is one of the most important and illusive points in the journey of completing a drawing. As soon as you cross the limit, your sketch will become a clumsy web of lines. The rule is to stick to the minimum and leave the areas other than the focal point unfinished and diffused. Details added all over the drawing will produce a flat picture. So start with the overall shape, work towards the focal point and add details only when absolutely necessary. Even the focal point of your sketch should be finished keeping the depth factor in mind and minimising the number of lines.

Remember, a drawing is not a photograph. It contains your personal tastes, likes and dislikes.

Owl

Sitting posture of an Owl is more upright, so the circle meant for head should be placed further towards the top of the oval shape which forms the body. Carefully mark the curve of the neck now, as with this bird it is very crucial and presents an awkward angle. Now draw the chest line which should end towards the legs. Slowly and steadily work towards the beak. Use the side of the pencil lead. As you complete the front portion which is falling over the eyes and onto the beak, add the beak itself. Draw in the eyes now, leaving the white highlights. Now work around the eyes and add the circular formations. Draw the neck line now and leave it on the chest. Switch on to the wings and draw the top area which is like a flying bird and forms the boundary of the lower part of the face. Keeping in mind the direction of the strokes, finish the wing. At last pick up the line of the chest again and with a long sweep draw the front of the bird and the feet.

Owl

The second Owl has a different view. Eyes are less visible as the top of the head has covered a major part of it. Back and both wings are more open here. Of the front portion, only the lower part and the feet can be seen. Very carefully observe the body posture and the way all three are looking around. Apart from the anatomy, the body language of the bird concerned is very important.

Snow Owl

Most hunting birds have strongly-built bodies, sharp, curved beaks and long talons.

Food and natural habits play a very important role in shaping the body structure of a bird. Their eyes, beaks, posture and feet take shape correspondingly.

This Barn Owl has been drawn on a tinted paper and by the EEE lumograph pencil. We have applied very little pressure to create the soft tone. The dark tone is applied with more pressure but only where it is absolutely necessary.

This Owl has very soft feathers with small dotted type of texture. The emphasis is on creating the overall shape and dark, illuminated eyes. This can be achieved by making the eyes very dark but leaving the highlight sharp and focussed.

Barn Owl

These beautiful Ducks are painted in water colours. We have used four very simple steps to complete it. Draw the birds first in very simple shapes with a sharp pencil. Apply a thin coat of water, leaving the birds dry. While it is still wet, apply a very light tone of grey on some parts. The strokes should be in vertical, except under the Ducks, where a slight zig-zag pattern will suggest their body shapes.

Add more dark shades beneath the grass, then let it dry. Define the shapes of the Ducks by using light and middle tones, leaving white areas intact. Add details in line work using a fine brush. You can use middle and dark tones, leaving white parts as they are. Finish the painting by defining darkest areas and the parts around the focal point, which in this case, is the head.

Try to spot a Snow Owl the next time you are in the mountains. Its silent, ghostly flight gives its prey (usually snow hares and other rodents) no hint of its attack. You can attempt this picture using acrylic colours. Note the big, powerful claws, big eyes and large, feathery wings. After drawing the bird, we painted in the background in light middle tones typical of a fairly bright, moonlit night. Some deep shadows break the monotony and add solidity. It is a scene of contrasts, just as you would expect to see on such a night.

This beautiful hunting bird is descending to sit on a branch. The technique to create a powerful bird like this one here is to draw the span of the wings and the relative drawing of the body and head very accurately, even in the primary stage.

Bald Eagle

34

Here is another picture of Bald Eagle sitting on a branch and surveying the surrounding landscape. As you get more familiar and comfortable with the basic ovals and circles, go for a more direct type of drawing. Here we have blocked the bird by two long curves suggesting wings. Then we drew in the head and connected it with the main body. Beak and the tail have been added then and the legs in the end. We have used Upper Hand Grip and short strokes along the pencil's length to outline this bird. The tone on the wings and upper leg is done by moving the pencil across. Try it yourself and see what happens. You may not succeed first, but in the second or third attempt you certainly will have some positive result. And all what you need is small success at short intervals.

Golden Eagle

This big, sharp-eyed bird of prey is a hunter. Big hunting birds have slow but graceful flight and the Golden Eagle is the best among them. Mark the wide wingspan and proportionate body. Add the head, beak and tail. You can see there is a good gap between primary feathers of the wings; they look like fingers.

The Golden Eagle spreads its tail for better control, which also acts like a rudder to give direction to its flight. Once in the sky, it glides effortlessly till it spots its prey on the ground and dives for it.

Golden Eagle

The Head

The heads and features of these 6-feet tall, beautiful, flightless birds called Emu, from Australia, never cease to amaze us. The variety of postures and expressions is really wonderful. Try different approaches when drawing their heads. Sometimes, make a sketch using the bare minimum of lines, giving them direction to define shapes. Then go for a bold approach and finish the portrait in just a few strokes.

Now select another bird to draw and mix in other techniques. Add maximum detail around the point of interest. Some smudging here and there will add a dream-like quality to the sketch, with the bird seeming to emerge from the mist.

Emu

Peacock

Snow Owl

Vulture

Vultures are scavengers and their presence is always associated with death. Start with the circle and add a triangular suggestion of the beak, with its curved tip. Position the eyes and then draw other parts such as neck, with its scanty hair-like feathers. Now focus on the detail around the eyes and beak. Your strokes should follow the curvature of the head very closely. Capturing character in a portrait is really satisfying.

Condor

Ringneck Duck

Heads can be drawn in many ways. See the portrait given here and find out the difference. The Ibis and Cockatoo have been done in lines only. You can see there is absolutely no shades. The Ringneck Duck has more dark areas and pronounced features. The basic approach is the same. Draw the circular shape meant for the head, add the beak and the eyes. Finish the picture on this base in any way you like.

Scarlet Ibis

Cockatoo

42

Mallard Duck

Flamingo

The Mallard Duck and the Flamingo have very distinct and different features. The Duck has a very circular shape but the Flamingo's head is of triangular shape with its beak turned downwards in an awkward manner. But the common thing is that both these heads have been finished with minimum of lines.

Always mark the basic shape in simple but identifying lines first. Your bird should be recognisable even at this stage. Now define the bird and its texture more accurately as per the original picture. Nearly in all cases, the darkest parts are the eyes, the beak and the areas which fall directly opposite the source of light.

Crowned Crane

Sparrow Hawk

Pelican

Penguin

How would you draw a bird that doesn't have any feathers? These potbellied birds are found in Antarctica. Draw the oval shape but in a more upright position, add the circle for the head, then the beak and eyes. The main difference is with the wings. It should be drawn as if hanging downwards. Tail and feet should be touching the ground. Now fill in the dark tone first. Define the outline and add the middle tone afterwards. Contrast between the darkest and brightest should be very pronounced. These birds move like fat clowns, but once they are in the water, they swim at amazing speed.

46

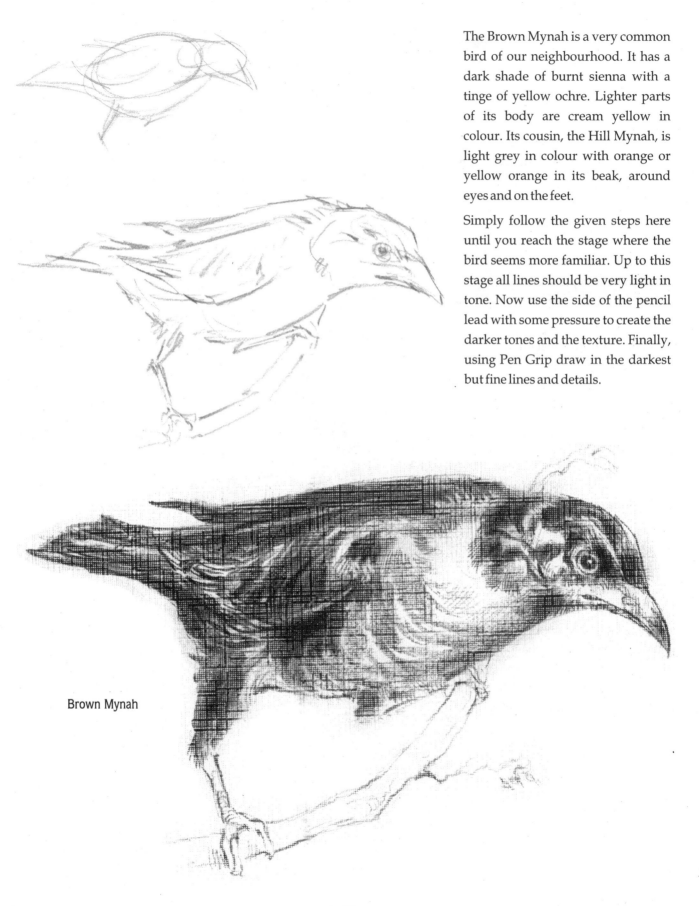

The Brown Mynah is a very common bird of our neighbourhood. It has a dark shade of burnt sienna with a tinge of yellow ochre. Lighter parts of its body are cream yellow in colour. Its cousin, the Hill Mynah, is light grey in colour with orange or yellow orange in its beak, around eyes and on the feet.

Simply follow the given steps here until you reach the stage where the bird seems more familiar. Up to this stage all lines should be very light in tone. Now use the side of the pencil lead with some pressure to create the darker tones and the texture. Finally, using Pen Grip draw in the darkest but fine lines and details.

Brown Mynah

African Crowned Cranes have round shaped bodies and very long necks and legs. It's really fascinating to see them moving. The slow, fluent movement of the head ends in a sudden jab as they capture their prey. Drawing them in pairs is a step further towards preparing a good composition for painting.

Start with placing an oval for the bird standing. Add the curved line for neck and place the circle for its head. Long lines for legs can then be added. Now do the same with the other bird. Remember that the more clearly and sharply you draw a figure, the closer it will appear to you.

Cranes drawn in groups present a good contrast of shapes. They have a good variety of heads with the standard frame of round bodies and long necks. Try to draw them when they are fighting, if you get the chance. Even the rough sketch will need very good speed. It surely will be difficult but it will improve your skill of drawing live models very much.

African Crowned Crane

African Crowned Crane

49

The Reference

Don't throw away that poor sketch of yours or that torn photo of a bird which you might have picked up from the road. Most successful persons are well informed, they say. That is especially true for an artist. Your stock of photos, drawings, videoCDs or books can make all the difference to the skill with which you work and the final outcome of a sketch. Take a small sketch book and a pencil along with you wherever you go. Whenever you get a chance, draw and make short notes of whatever you find interesting. Try copying the living things and the original objects, not the picture. Write down the name, colour or anything notable. Within a short period you will have your own reference library.

Barn Swallow

Robin

These small Roadrunners run very fast. We have tried here the direct approach of sketching. Observe the bird for a while before you start drawing it. Draw the finish lines directly without any help of the basic shapes. It is a very good practice to gain efficiency in drawing live birds.

Roadrunner

Ring-necked Pheasant

The wings become prominent when we draw a flying Pheasant. Always mark the body first, only then add the graceful outlined shape of the wings to it otherwise you will lose the relative proportion. Now draw the head, the line for the neck and the triangular shape of the tail. Check the texture on the feathers and the tail very carefully and then start finishing as per the original picture. The different directions in which the wings spread and the feet turn are important, so keep them in mind while completing the drawing.

Ruffed Grouse

53

Peacock

To draw this beautiful bird, first you need to study it very carefully. You soon will find that it is a combination of many different birds. The main body is of oval shape like Duck, the neck is long but the curve is like that of Pigeon. The legs remind us of the Cock.

So, first draw the oval shape and a long sweeping line for back and tail. Draw the triangular outline of the head and the crown-like features. Connect it with main body as shown in step one. Add the lines indicating legs and the lower part of the tail. Add some shade on the neck and some texture on the wing and tail. Start finishing everything in detail now, keeping the original picture in front of you. Draw it in detail as shown in the main picture and also with minimum of lines as in small sketches. There is no other way to master it.

The Peacock is one of the most beautiful birds. Its feathers reflect all the colours of the rainbow. It walks very gracefully, bobbing its head and neck. In the rainy season, it dances with its tail spread into a fan-like formation which is a lovely sight to see. It is not a strong flier. It is India's national bird.

Peacock

Swifts are the fastest flying birds in the world. The Spine-tailed Swift can touch a top speed of 106 miles per hour. These tiny creatures can go through the sky with amazing speed.

All the lines and the body parts indicate the direction where the bird is heading. Give an overall middle tone first before finishing it with dark details.

Spine-tailed Swift

56

Frigate Birds fly with a fast, rhythmic, flowing movement. You should see them when they snatch fish from the beaks of other birds; they do it in mid-air!

The male Frigate Bird is a glassy black with a red throat pouch. They move in groups and are slow on the ground, but once in the air, they are hard to match.

Frigate

Draw an imaginary centreline which starts from the head and goes through the body, along the spine and up to the end of the tail of the bird. Now place the oval shape for the body and other basic parts on this centreline. You will find the drawing more balanced. Now add the final outline and the main texture to create this beautiful bird. When drawing many birds in a group, always keep the relative proportion of their bodies correct as per their position.

Ring-necked Pheasant

59

Puffin

These birds have also been drawn in the manner we have described in the Eagle's drawing. The difference is in the posture of the birds. Puffin is sitting in a more upright position like the Eagle so it should be drawn in the same way. The Nightjar is sitting more horizontally with the earth. So the circle of head should be placed more sideways in the primary drawing. The pattern of finishing is same.

King fisher

Eagle

Sometimes we use round type of strokes, without lifting our pencil or breaking the lines. It is fun and we strongly recommend that you try it. On this primary jumble of suggestive lines, as shown here, we have directly drawn the final sketch of this beautiful Eagle. The darkest parts are the eyes, centreline of the beak, lower part of the wings and the tail.

Shearwater

Some birds like the Albatross and Shearwater can stay in the air for very long periods. Take care to keep the proportions of the body and the wings correct. Note how closely they resemble that of a glider. Knowledge of primary and secondary feathers is of great help when drawing outspread wings.

Drawing birds in flight is always a source of excitement for us. Due to their different sizes and shapes, birds produce a variety of poses when in flight. Correct drawing of wing span and the placement of the flying bird in your working area is very important.

Osprey

It Never Ends.......

Hornbill

Drawing and painting is a passion, once you get into it. With the passing of time, the interest may change from one subject to another, but the hobby remains. It is one of the surest ways to get name, fame and, of course, money. Above all, you will get immense pleasure in drawing your favourite subject. Once you get the taste of bringing something excellent on your paper from nowhere, you will get stuck to it, for life. Drawing does have a beginning as a hobby but surely has no end, so keep moving that pencil of yours.

Water Hen